"Everything about Carolyn Srygley-Moore's latest collection of poems underscores and emphasizes her wish to provide hope and refuge: the stark and beautiful black and white pictures; the light font; leading; and white space allowing the poems plenty of room to breathe; her acknowledgement to those able to survive 2023; the opening Dickinson epigraph to hope. And, of course, the poems. Srygley-Moore's work is known for fearlessly chronicling horror, but here she is more often found compassionately embracing the landscape, or offering a forgotten victim the chance of repentance. *"Parking Lot Poems"* may well be a desert-island book, not just because it is so good to preserve when all other books vanish, but because with Srygley-Moore as our spirit guide, we can escape any desert island on which we are imprisoned."

-Loring Wirbel, poet, author

"These poems are shocks of light from fireflies, stars, and gunfire across the parking lot of our lives. Carolyn Leigh Srygley searches through the smoke signals and matters of soul we dwell in to illuminate the "walls between my heart and the howl" with an honest and experienced compassion."

- Jared Smith --Author of T*he Shoebox at the End of The Universe* (Stubborn Mule Press)

"In her new collection, *Parking Lot Poems*, Carolyn Leigh Srygley offers reflections on justice, cruelty betrayal. Her minimalist imagery can at times appear chaotic, hesitant on the page – perhaps reflecting the chaotic reality humans have created. She speaks of the frailties, the failures of humanity as she writes for "the vulnerable ones." Carolyn asks the reader to question "what suffering is necessary." In *Untitled*, Carolyn declares "you don't need my distant words"….."there is never a reason to bomb babies." In another Untitled, her frustration is stark "have they turned on the damned water." Carolyn's latest collection asks the hard questions. Her readers must find their own answers."

-Sharon SingingMoon, author of *Random Seed* &
The Weight of One Hummingbird Feather

"Even before I read the first poem, the title of Carolyn's new collection had me thinking about Joni Mitchell's *Big Yellow Taxi*, paving paradise for a parking lot. Like in the song, we often don't know what we have 'til it's gone; she speaks to that loss, inviting you to ditch your car altogether and spend the evening in reflection. I read these poems as expressions of both grief and gratitude with line breaks serving as both stabs and salves. From Traces (we have all lived in hell awhile) to Pigeons (If someone anywhere somewhere/believes in you/makes all the difference) to Everywhere (we can be kind/we can be good), you will recognize your humanity here."

-Julie Miller, MLS

PARKING LOT POEMS
(reflections)

Poems by Carolyn Leigh Srygley

Kung Fu Treachery Press

Rancho Cucamonga, CA

Copyright © Carolyn Leigh Srygley, 2024
First Edition: 1 3 5 7 9 10 8 6 4 2
ISBN: 978-1-958182-58-1
LCCN: 2023952132

Cover photo and title page image: Jon Lee Grafton
Author photo: James Srygley-Moore

Acknowledgments

George, "the Social Scientist," Jason Ryberg / anyone who survived the year 2023 With capacities for love & living Intact; Bynx, forever, of course; the Brain surgeons at Albany Med & My friend Rashid, the Neuro- ICU aide, as relevant to my survival as the surgeons. Thank you all.

Table of Contents:

For James.

'hope is the thing with feathers that perches in the soul...'
— Emily Dickinson

LIGHT, BREAKING

Black water thick
      Firefly wick reflections here //
Over there // if I could hear
Light breaking at light's speed
I'd hear little gasps &
Echoes tumbling in stacks pushed
To fall like dominoes shining
     Gashing dark.

The water thick;
Where are the architects my brothers
    & beings
Of bridge, threshold, compass?
The island is comfortable
     A room
Heated mildly in portent
Of a hard winter.

  I've moved more than once.

Boundary, an illusion.
Little bells of October, fireflies
Died off days ago.
These are broken ghosts
In the sea, spirits of yesterday & tomorrow, flagellum,
    Blood-flares.

DESPITE
(ambrosia) despite

Spooning the flesh
Of oranges
    A halved shell

Grey
Tap water plink plink
        Potato peel
    Fragments

Thunk iron.
        I recall
    Cooking
Together
   June nights —. Or it was

Winter —

Husking corn into the daily news
Headlines smudged .
       Yet
Blinders &

    Not- knowing
Kept us awake at night
The wait

The dropping cadence
    Harvests
Recalled. Dammit you

I'm just waiting
For humidity to break
Waiting
    A late night rainfall
Sprinkling coconut & cinnamon
To save
    Our little world.

LOVING

Padding barefoot around sleeping
Cats on moon pillows
Heating her formula (then)
Your tea (now)

I love touching your shoulder

So lightly
That you do not startle
But turn
My way
    Your face opening

I love to empty my skirt pockets before
    You

    Show the apple switchblade
I no longer carry

 Currently
A cut silhouette

An imprint in the wall.

TRACES

I read your silences
I hold them near as my own breasts
  Are near the tick of carotid
      A dove coo at the window

The roof water trickles
  Just where an electric bulb swings
      Bare from an orange string
The moonlight floods & tickles
  Sudden

I am without breath
Without death.
I've nothing to lock myself against.

      Hey I've lived in hell awhile
        I trust you have too

& I'm telling you — remember?
      Spaces are close stink & sweat
          Distance of a gnat wing between
        That unnerving disco glitter
Dizzy as a gin hangover
  The rank of sweat & rue.

STEPPING OUT

It's not just

Addiction, survival, pump to the vein

    No
Empire
No near skyscraper
Within length of an arachnid crawl.

    Diaries signify hue. Maybe
Hue only

        Ghosts uncoil fog
Calligraphy from the page
It is not frail like

Holy parchment —

    Aspiration feeds on spirit
      Strong spirit
        Blood & spit
Muscle spirit
& spits it out upon the page again .

    Omniscient no
A
Humanity spills

"If it was only tribal
Divided
"All too
Human"
There'd be no point
Attempting
Love & cadenced worlds.

NOT GALLOWS (to speak of)

On the other side
Of innocence, the painter
Shows us watercolor runaway
Canoes mounting grit

Mount
Like twinned trees — not
Gallows —
That are the perch
Of balsa
Owl house, to nest, be
Nest,
Get accustomed
To /gather
Biting petals   winter wind.

There occurs
Near dust infiltrating sundown a brief
Exchange:
About giving away
All poems
Sketches
Paintings
We will complete.   an ellipsis
Granted
A mama
Elephant's trunk

Curling up & over

    Her calves that they might

Know
What
Freedom is.

CONSIDERING THE PASSAGE OF LIGHT

Monet traveled
South,
Monday afternoons
 A sandwich & wine
  Sun at his side

  Seeking a different molecular
  Quality

Light

  Fractured as it fell
  Upon blades of

Water / lily pad / petal...
 Lens of cloud or clarity

 & the conjecture of seasons//
The passage — written
& unwritten

Honest
 History through portrait haystacks

 —

 Time through the natural
World. He stood near
Museum
 Landscape

Paintings
    As a boy — aware —
        Each stroke rising thick
  Slight
Above canvas —.

    He was an epiphany

  Dwarfed by no impasse
Between the present & possibility —
The fact of the austere yet
Forgiving
  Physical
The natural world.

       (Or so I imagined at 15
        When I'd look @ a Monet

RIDING THE LOOP

(For Charlotte)

Glad to consider
It all a dot a dash.
Simple
    Smoke signals

Erupt from sidewalks
& alleyways
Sloughed
    Presence

Not of the dead // but of the missing.
O man. 9 year old
Girls & boys
    Riding the bike loop

Or the father gunned down
In the warehouse
Just by
    The President's house —:

I send a friend poems
He sends me photographs
Of milk cartons
    & I swear

I've had conversations with them all.
Perhaps we have become them all.

PIGEONS

The unsayable
   Lurks like a sooty green street pigeon
     Amidst wilderness leaves
       October
Lurks between ice skate cuts
   In lake slate layered thick &
     A drugged moon's wake

If someone anywhere somewhere
Believes in you
   Makes all the difference

   Mercy

How the mythical
   Muscular tongue &
Gavel
   Land.

NOW GHOST

A bicycle trail laces the oblique lake
A fishing pier now closed —:

Just as neon's dawn recedes
   Colors smash
     Bashed
Damn upstate trees of
Mid-October
     I pull tires upon the margin
& step upon the aluminum bridge
   Making landfall
      Where marshy rot
Ends.   Outlet Road & Lakeview closed & black
Dog now ghost
Stand
   The pier buoyant
     A helium balloon basket

     A still & porous anchor
Everything
   Moving dizzily dizzily faster.

SCARED OF SHADINGS

The mob
Chants then sifts to ash
Like flour.
    How many stones
Have you skipped
Across shadow wakes of the river?
    How many stone throws
Boomerang against the red bandit
Autumn breeze.

Harvest, face of moon
Forms. A painter I loved briefly
As a dart nipping
    Ephemeral
Told me — often — the contrast
Of light against shadow
        Forms the physical
World, the flesh & bone, tables & chairs
On which the blind depend.

What
He said
Are you afraid of.

DYLAN'S HARMONICA

A blue harmonica fades in
& out
  Moon song waxing
Waning.   Shifts
Gently seismic.
  What you count on.
I wish I was that harmonica

  One tool one set of
Perforations
By any name —
  What changes us absolutely—

(Tide crashes upon the blackout jetty)

(Older still, we are straddling the blackened
    Jetty)

(Someone's carrying us home)

INFUSED

She lay upon a mattress
Feeling the pea, lungs black rough as
   Gaughin's teeth; knows
Every word every finger snap Sinatra
Sings for her, ballads
 Personal.

They say that song is that last to go. Yea
   Doctor

Song goes last, climax, denouement.
   A trail of laughter—

Petals scattered
 Yellow petals infused.

DEPARTURES

God left. I was 11
Slammed the trapdoor

Sneaky moonlight
Padding the player piano
Keys.

Hymn
Gutted carefully
Scalpel & surgeon & lens
Deft corded monitors we are caught
Just
At the flatline

Beep

I was 7
I was 3

(Once. I walked
A house thick with photographs
Burnt or scissored or in
Dense baby book piles razored

& all I can see is a bit of sea
Foam displaced like broken rib
On a glass that I planned
On washing tonight)

My mouth is open
I'm gulping tap water
I'm thinking how great it is
Having clean cold water.

PRIVILEGE

(After "A Room of One's Own"
-Virginia W)

Always had
   A space
Walls kept or challenged
  always a window.
   Alley / creek / piano
      Floating in a vegetable garden
From which deer
Came & went.

Books
The living & the dead
   Scattered amidst
     Sheets

Postcards
Taped to the screen
Zen black branching
  Kept fiercely.

Always had a place
Of my own
The molten clockwork
The cadenced cog.

Visitors
& night falling into rivers
From breaking graffiti
   Forgetting

How sacred the body
How intricate
Its corridors its milked walls.

READING KAFKA IN LAUNDROMATS

Big deer eyes glint wet

Lay the brittle mosaic;
What cannot be spoken.

""

     What should be spoken.

"Why was I locked in winter
My thin nightclothes
Bitten by the howl"

""

When home is
A laboratory experiment—
     An observation tower

"Will the child follow
The laser with its wincing gaze"

"How does the white coat respond
To bed wetting "

"How does the white coat respond
To instinct & self-comforting
     Masturbation"

""

Xxxxx

""

This is where we learn
The hunger artist

This is where we learn
The uncanny
        Endurance

The traveler
Who does not travel

The
    Lifting of gavel.

TRANSPARENCY

She says in prisons
    Midst murderers
        She feared singing of death
Afraid it might
Inspire someone
But she sang, anyway .
(She says
"What makes the holy triangle
But that man, present, who knows what
    Murder is")

""

Somewhere monks chant
& as they plant & bulb & seed
The sky rain is their avalanche
This tumble of funhouse mirrors.
(She says
"The prophets moan too
       as lovers
   &&
Murderers moan.")

FREEDOM

He said the word today

As if he owned it; a plum pit nested

   In the tongue curl
      That white-dimpled muscle.

SALT
CHILD
SCRATCH

            & courageous or silly

I took that word
            Frustrated

Because nobody owns language

   Just as the sea
      Lapping water of the pink

Nude

Beach

      FIGURES
       CIRCLE
      DANCE THE TREE DOWN.

YOU WERE NOT THERE

(Response to David Gray's Skellig)

I'm trying to recall traveling to
Islands
   It has happened
Although you were not there

   Don't tell
Me the stink of brine & rotting
       Dolphin arc
Did not strike my heart

Did not occur.
       When they saw open
The human skull
So little is there
   Holding the lobes together

       & traveling this
   Space between the world
& a mass of rock & sand
       I've seen

Faces of people I've loved
Yet never meant to love & hey

       It's not as hard to watch
   Oneself
Destroyed

As it is
To watch the others. & baby
Stunned
    Like a pigeon
Struck
By what it thought is sky

Mercy is
A wingspan like the breadth of a hand

Only human.
    Been lowered into that table
Of ether
Wanting only a glass of water
To sip
To gulp
To carry.

THE SPECIAL MOAN

For James

Not an apple
    Not the pitched splayed
Tongue of a woman
Not the honeymoon from violence before
Brother
Screwed it up —

What makes it possible
Is that head tilt
 Place at your neck
  Back
    Where
Greying hair mats
How you always forget to shave
   Your face the round of it
      I glimpse
   Your skin gleaning
The color of sunset mauve.
How you say yea
Your laugh
    Caught in your breath
Like a tiny
  Gestating
  Moan.

BEWITCHED

For Russel, 1980

The scroll
 Calligraphic black
Floral along the edges.

 Asking "will you let me
Lay this blade to your skin, drink
You?"

 Tick tock
Raindrop
 Pages stank
Sudden
Of
Turpentine

 "Can I have walls please
Between my heart
& the howl."

JAILBREAK

General X
    It's said
Was trapped on the battlefield

Of massacre; glimpsed
Going to & fro

Amidst the rot before bone

""

Remorse
    I consider
Comes & stays
Comes & goes

Or transmutes to a halo
    Unholy the holy
Filthy slag heap history

""

J & I
Stayed up one night

—. streetlamp click we stirred from
The zone

Discussing

Remorse & history

Transcending
  Jailbreak
      // rain-struck orange
Dawn.

NOSTALGIA

Words inhabit snow dunes drifting

        Can't catch each living curl
    Of ink

Or graphite used to tattoo
    Crosshatch

 Thighs of the pale
Ballerina

    Words, drifting

Beautiful monsters under bed
    Rather

Baby rattle dust bunnies rolling

& webs carrying fat sacs
    Baby spiders blue-

Torched by delinquents

All
The things I wish I didn't know

(The taste of her)

    Baby I

Fall falling
Keep away from the edge
Yet I dance here every instant

All things dizzy
(Dolphin mobile spinning

The ether table).

All the things
What I should have done

What I said
Without sense of consequence

O baby

Nostalgia

Has little to do with the dead.

RESOLUTION

When x died
The dogs stopped barking
The halved howls of wolves

Time silenced itself — an automatic
Borne by a man
Who'd forgotten who he was.

      They said the house
  Once a hotel
Drifted
From the beginning — ribcage
  & esophagus

Heavy with voices
Woke the night
Having lived & come back

Once again, simply set
Roses & chocolate cherries at rest
On pillows of want & walls.

ALWAYS, TRAVELERS

"""

      Who goes before
  Whom is never known —

You said
I'd head out before
    You, here I am
Wrapping you to a mummified legacy
Drip drop embalming
Fluid

  Here I am, never wanting to
Outlive
You, or you, or my friend you—: fog bank
Figure, spit out your hidden trickster
    Imps & misread stars
The doe eclipsed so she is dead
      Yet love not gone.

JESTS OF THE FALCON

Mirror on mirror on love-me-not mirrors.
I did not fall
    In, nor look too close

    Flushed &
        Stunned by mirage.
Will it be

It will be
    Long before I'm taught
To hold a song-note past a finger snap!
Just trying to learn
    The preparation.

"

 Mirror on mirror, gutted
& how often does the falcon jest

    The yellow lure. Tell me.
        Hush & whisper

I bear the chord raw bleeding tests
As this // pressure

On the carotid, I gag
On happiness, this, bled-berry stain

    Hushabye

Paint,
Hunter & the hunted
     Love-me-not todays
Tire me, never enjoyed the numbing
Kiss
  Uncut cocaine.

SURVIVOR, MOON

Coming back to this place
Parthenon length pools, statues flesh

   Jimmy
& Donna

Who — fighting — hobbled in & out,
To & fro, wincing like arthritic
   Heavens in their pain/

Or joy, was it. Moon, a song
Calls it killer, I call it rescuer, dropping
Now

   Into a shroud of givens,

The poplar maple oak
Red & shedding
     Guardian
   Rainbow hounds.

THE ANONYMOUS ONES

Electric blades whirr & whirring
Stir the sweat of winter

& the memory of
Wings .
         Nothing like
Dropping something
   On marketplaces ;
         Something whistles in my head

Said dad in his blue plaid
Suede circles
Stitched to the elbow.

""

Faces
Form somehow," he said
   "Rise like teacup & saucer
Hover, spacecraft "

   He tended bar
& after a shift 6 am to
Closing tried to just hang out

A bit. But the disparate
Floated & winked —. tigers in light

"Dislocated mouths, moans."

"."

Remorse
Irreconcilable

Lantern & gut thread & goggles —
Sewing kit
    The anonymous pilot

Grafting name to the anonymous dead
Grafting skin to kitchen-cat faces.

"."

    Wing or fist
Says the 3 am moon,
Asking at least
Wing
                & name.
Just one of each would do.

SEIZURE CONTINUUM

"Ran out for some groceries
Tinned pork, oil sardines. Tobacco
Blocks of dark chocolate anything
To carry us through
      Hesitation."

Small village, recently
Paved roads.
Where court meets Galway
   A time craft in the cellar
A spacecraft for
      The burned

Syringes for the astronaut
Who did not
Want to return
   Having seen the globe blue & gold
Spinning spinning spinning

A seizure that enters continuum

   (A drunkard retching
  Nobody holding her hair back

     An addict
Tossed back as the junk
Hits
  Shitting
As she hits the damned yet surmountable wall.

IMPERFECT SAND

"They're only castles burning".

-Neil Young

"""

Wish I could sleepwalk
    shut
Off,
      Zone.

    A couple people
A world
      walking
In their sleep, riptide ripples

Blurry yet

"Only in dying are we omniscient "
Or so whisper

  The once-breathless

Still full of rattling soul pits, red
    Plum &
Rice grains
      Piñata pinks of an afterlife.

Old friend
Anne woke once
    On a ledge,

Wobbled a bobble head

Cowgirl
  & snap
Went the hypnotist
Fingers.

           But truly
       Nobody ever woke into a perfect

  Ellipsis & so
We

              Float, wisp
Between this & that
   Here & there, a capsule
Anonymous
      Sandbox dew.

SKETCH (of a mother)

Climbing out of a suburban
    Mini-Van
A very thin woman
   Loiters around the back
Seat
Door.
    She brushes a piece of beige hair
  From the curve of
Her cheekbone
        Throws her head
Back slightly
Face turned to the pancake sky
  Peering through haze.
As if in slow
Motion
   An instant of smudged
Weariness in her eyes
Vague &
Narrow
   A bit of dread
Perhaps for the future

& I'm certain there is a small
Child waiting

    A presence before which
    She pauses
Gathering stance
Before the truly

Vulnerable ....
& a door opens
    & the woman's face opens
        As if the child is a daily
Surprise.

SINGING CRADLES

Just a guy, a red painted harmonica
    Tangled grey ponytail
 A guitar

One guy on a stage

Built of a broken down falcon wing
Or '72 rice field
Bamboo
    Cage.

Someone calls "buddy"
His head turns
Remembering all the faces
The places
Cradle & crèche & pebble —:

    Red harmonica

Echo & vigilance

(What poem would you recite
    Just when you know
        You're dying)

        Tattoos
That are faces / lucky numbers
    Angels & Satan alike

A hollow dark echo wet
The grainy call
Guitar   as walls
Tumble.

HOMESICK (for you who are

I don't write about words
I leave unspoken
    Those creatures I love —
I don't speak of you
Lisping vow to vow soft
Of silences
    Champagne bottles smashed
To flint & syllable
On the shipwrecked bow.
    I don't speak
Of red
The pomegranate tea we steep
In sundown
    On the tenth acre
    Of land
We call our own.

Privileged we till stone & clay
Brittle as kilned
Memories
    Rising to the surface
    We plant
Digging bowls of mud
For rooting
    We plant bouquets for the people
Who have no land
Not even
A bit of a wall
    To call a house
    A home

A room with a door
To
Latch or leave unlatched.

The dogs stir, are stirring
Me from thoughts of the
You
        Of whom I'll never speak
Or know
As the loon just across the water,
Yet must
Keep
Safe
        A word on the tongue's pink
    Inner curl.

CLEANING THE PORCH

Rooting
Dark corners, old porch
I find
   An envelope
Addressed to me — within,
Taped

   A key: what knob fit —
What door —
What summer camp trunk
   Now, bottom
Caved in , the damp of old porches.

     Out spill
   Snippets of thought
That I valued, enough to write them
In an old thin ruled ledger,
Yellow / things I once thought
To be

     Matters of science linked
   Mysteries
  Matters of soul.

SUDDEN

A barn owl
Homed in the kitchen window. I told
You, that is our guardian
Calling calling
From the axis
Of folklore. These tales
You urge to me
Rattling midst spoons &
   Water glasses urge
As fact
As truth

& baby ruthless as our tongues
Are, can be,
I trace you back
A bar full of kicked in jukeboxes
Playing songs about granite bridges
& seagulls like old comrades laughing
Going round & round
Kindred of voice & of soul.

GROUNDED

The woman
   Circular blue kitchen
Transfixed by a grasshopper
Big eyes big eyed
   Itty bitty kangaroo.
She tossed a salad
Brown lettuce peeled away
  From the good near center
    The thick core pounded
Baby cucumber skin forest green
        Just
    Picked. Fruit stand

A person who's floating a little
Like the posture of a
   Violinist
     Androgyne breasted

  Thinned down oil
The stink of turpentine , waking
Smudges pastel
  Green. Hands
On.
     Core the apple 1
   2
3
Husk the corn silk
  Threads

Hands
ON.

**** transition *****

"""

WHISPERS IN THE WHISKEY (I didn't / don't
want to write another war poem.)

"
       I hear
Whispers
All the demolished bridges:
    Women split apart by men
        That favorite instrument
            Like highway deer by semis

(Must be like leaving your body
When the pain hits
& you realize what it is.
        Mute
Being buried
        Alive

By the depth & shovel
Of your own
        Scream.)

"

Just takes a minute
To hurt

Step out upon the fragile edge
  Seeing
        Being
The dehumanized/ dehumanizing

Marionettes — passive, active—
& even if you cut
The effin' strings
        They've been told
    Since origin
What their reality of love & hatred must be.

""

O robot
O machine

The Simon Says
The chanting breadline
The Simon Says
Carousel birthday party & games
Suck you in / spit you out
        Games.

""

    Fragmented, whispers.
Blood is same
    / We are not all the same

Our landscape
Identical
    Before the beginning

Only at the beginning.

All those razors sharpened

All those razors along wrists
  Pale
Of endurance//

  Love

I'm only the fragile edge
Of what a being
Is
      Watching snowflakes thud
The death of summer.

TURNING OFF THE BREATH

Voices
In the street, jabbing
       Silence

— : What is refuge

Turn off the slight wheeze a breath
   Forces, even a newborn's soft
Inhale

—: What is disposable

& science declares
That even silence makes its own noise,
   A deadly
Clatter

—: What is the broken shadow

A safety pin hydroplaning on a
   Puddle black & red

—: can't be heard
   Though they are screaming

HAZE FROM NYC (electric eels)

If i squint
   So many raindrops
Slash
   Love-me-please
Petals

   Syllables
Words smashed open
   The geodes mauve global sundown
Against stunted
Trees
   Squint

Difficult to see

 Across New York smogs
   Struck deer
      &
The briny
Waters
            Brevity
Of infinity

Dwarfed
   By
Bloodletting on
      An alternate
Screen.

UNTITLED

A young woman

Takes her face apart
On lunch break
  In clattering figments
Grease paint & iron

"''"

The romance,
The rumors…
  Something about onyx swans
In the palace pond
& the sculpting of David —

"''"

Creative/ destructive

She takes her face apart. Eyes
The khaki of camouflage.

"''"

Considers:
  Stephen
    Dug
Out his eyes for he had been told

He lusted with
His soul & surely.

"""

Lust was ethical sometimes
Somehow, could start a story
Somehow, & evoke

Empires made of sugar //

It was the violence that screwed it up.

"""

   O damn lunch
Break was done
Filaments

    Flashed
Citrus
& she's forgotten to eat the
Sandwich he'd fixed for her
A kiss & a day ago.

UNTITLED

Sirens intercept our conversation
Occasionally
We largely use back roads
Avoiding impasse
Breaking the artery

  Cut into stone
Red clay Rosetta code
Our fissured catacomb —;
No. Yes
It never eludes
Me, leaf leaning
Tip lightly
Penetrating wind
What bird & plane use

To drop shit
On the blanched face looking up —
Faces, children
Reading a picture book
Mouths ajar.

ANYWHERE

We sat at a small town bistro
Iron wrought table   Chairs
Corner of Front & Court.
Almond scones, black coffees.
People milled about us. Small
Mobs or disparate threads
Fragrant, stinking.
It was a close space. Sadist
Tommy was showing in
The Park; projected
Like a home movie
On a statue, granite, nearly crawling
With fat crows. Hooded birds: "they are
Migrants" you said " Just birds".
I thought —
Proof
That we have souls at least &
The throngs human
Around us shrilled. "Everyone sounds
The same" I said
" at least when they scream."
"Somewhat" you said
Tipping your Yankees baseball cap " except
When they're singing."

LOVING THE BASS

Hounds of rescue
Gather on winter terraces

Children in thin gowns
Gather in the howl

& a tall man
Throttles his bass

As a woman in red
Clings

Her violin bow chipping
Fingernail clippings

A manicurist stage left.
A man fired me

From that place of kneeling
Emptied of knowledge

My yellow raincoat
No hint of either heaven or

The other side
Of the river.

How can you choose
The death of another

Gasping for water
How can we choose

Mountains breathing
Cargo & eggshells cracking

Yes. How can we breathe
Shine into eyes of the newborn.

How can we

During it

Before it

After it ——. Breathe.

APOLITICAL

Yellow hazmat gear
   Ash in sieve
Sifting

   Electromagnetic waves
Over plaid flannel sheets

  The mummy seeks witness
  A soul shifts
  Traversing
  Sundial its curves of darkness

Have you
In your thin memoir
   Slept with fingerprints
    Kept in
Bathrobe pockets
Merely a speckling whorl

Nibbling aphrodisiac lettuce
Wet with river fresh
Acquires ecstasy

Over the Hudson
Transcended
Translating
  The Nile.

THE COMEDY

Starlings & dogs chase
Light & fat flying red
Squirrels dart
    Dodge
Oncoming traffic quick quick
Seeming immortal. We see

    A red squirrel
Displaced from its woodland
— as a kid I'd watch
Them alight on trees by my brother's
Library tower —:

    Thunk, struck by
Unseen launches rocketing
Skyscraper or shades
Of fog in ether —
Curls like a dying bumblebee

    & kisses its black toes
Slow
    As if saying hello.

UNTITLED (at essence)

Did they turn on the water

"

Can wax figures
Contain the human
Will

"

Did they turn on the water

"

In the heat
Of exile & exodus
Eye melts to
Nose the
Mouth as gateway occluded

"

Did
They
Turn
On the water

"

Y holds my dog near
To his ribs
As he speaks of a childhood
In Lebanon
& how he was trained to cure

H draws blood from my
Pit-bull who is dying
Slow of lymphoma
& says "I am
Jewish; I have been to Israel " she nods
Slightly

The stranger at
The church where we loiter
Without memory of belonging
Says "it's good

We visited Jerusalem last year
    Instead"

& I am futile

"

I'm suddenly angry
Outraged

"

Did they turn on the water

"

In a twilight episode
The wax figures light wick
& reconfigure faces

"

Did they

"

&
The will to act
Engages the will

Involuntary
As the aortic flap
Or lung black
Cilia's flutter

The will to yield.

"

Have they
Turned on the damned
    Water

UNTITLED

You don't need my distant words
They are supplicant irrelevant
Conversations
Salted like grits with butter

Granules of sweet

You don't need thrift shop
Witnessed acts & obligations
encountered // held
Down
(Or hand upon you
Raised —
Lifted —)

Eventually
Gravity itself
Bombarded

Houses & what seems steadfast //
A porch railing//
Upside down

Lunch is
Rot in a lunch bag
All is
Ditch &
A front //
Is it

Child
Is there / there is
     "Never a reason
          To bomb babies"
The
Paused comic says (lost his dad
In 9/11)

Never a season
          To hunt // Immolate
The unwilling unknowing

Ones.

HOW LONG CAN WE BE SILENT

"Can't hold your breath
Til you die"

They say
But I wiggle-swam the length
Of the wet chasm between
    Scratching shadows
Teeth bare as a tiger green
Eyed
    Fangs exposed
— needing the necessary
        Fresh

I sipped the salt
& brine

Breathed.

            Hoping
        A flask of bourbon mixer
Human fear
Could slay the thirst
    Manifold
            Of they who pursue
    Quietly
Canteens

Comprehension //
Vulnerability gutted blue

That dusk's carrion feed

Breathe.

DOGS KNOW

Bloodhounds scramble

Rescue
     Some humanity
With each snuffle each
Head tilt
     Belly crawl home
Through inimitable
     Shadows scratching

     Lust & treason
Fantasy & unreason —:

Such is

Anatomy of blasts &
     Bullet holes.   For all who
Like the great shark
Move
     In order to keep on
          Breathing

     Without drama
("Look away")
     ("Fill the clay vase with water")
          ("Scrub your face of ash & tears") yea

Honey
    this is how
It's
Done.

WHAT HE SAID

What he said.

"There are no innocents "
He said, pulling
Feather barb
From curved shaft —

    Like petals

A hooded crow winces
  Dreamt invincibility

The darkest shade of blue —:

& we walked
Pasture stretching vast green

& hot rubble

Walked coal lines arranged by thumbs
With no print //

    Disciplined
  To disregard

Soothsayers
    Of each noose thrown
  Like fabled urban stone
& fire

ALLIES

(For Jack Varnell my friend)

Met you somewhere midair

"Could've been a better person "
You said —:

"Maybe not killed yourself
    In your mother's home."

""

Wasn't right,

3 days,
    Blue bully jays clattered
        Louder than thrown
    .   Furniture

"

Outside
    Deck stones flower
  As moons flower

Moss flourishes
Scrape scrape the old woman
    Says; that would

Kill the red chipmunk she says;

Kill the dancing spiders.

I love spiders, rainbows of spiders.
  So many windows

""

Even the blue jays lurking in blueberry bushes wouldn't
  Be that
    Candid.

I didn't mean to murder
  Self, her, anyone; the dreams sometimes
    Of others.   Surely

The tambourine// the harmonica

""

If the love doesn't figure it out
Nothing will

      Surmounting the drones.

TO BE REAL

Nothing was mirage
About it — lovemaking
                Lean gazelles
        Chance graced carnal
Encounter

    Then birds of prey, we were

    Afloat in a planetarium

Yet stars burned real

    The brevity of saxophones

A finger snap
            A
Cigarette ground
With a boot heel
On the Gettysburg flame.

GINGER TEA

I glimpse you here &
There

    Walking amidst cedars jumbling
Woodland pattern

Perhaps it is only a shadow
Long with bowls of buttock & skull
    Dressed in the greatest organ

    I call your name
I call you out yes

I glimpse you now & then
    A fragile charcoal thread smudged
    Where the lines are marked

By points
    Interfering with infinity

Leaf spiraling along currents of autumn
Like wings of a cardboard bird
    Earthbound by someone's birdbath

    Honey
    I put on a kettle
The back door is unlatched

Let's share some red mugs
The bite of steaming
  Ginger tea

ORDINARY // we each weep

Blood

The sky
  Scarlet tourniquet
Incomparably
      Uncertain

    Gash
  Certain
Occurs

  Love & hatred
Each
Riot
& root

Where the scarlet
Games
    Play

A creature
Flawed // earnestly flawed

  Hooks the saline drip

An incidental

Cyanide

Drip

    The ordinary
Distracted by a sandwich
& a too human
Hunger

      Ordinary

How the blank eyed
    Snap necks
  Of chickadee & hen

Or chance
    Bedouin

EVERYWHERE

It's everywhere
Geese gathered in pastures
Prepared to fly.

Sometimes they mob the crosswalk
& cordoned vehicles
Stop traffic to let them pass.

& we can be kind, people.
& we can be decent

Shielding our eyes
By the Working Farm
    Lamb & turkeys fattened

Gathering by a gate
To be
    Watered & fed.

We can be kind.
We can be good.

REACHING

"You've been put on the world to love the act of being alive."

—Ray Bradbury, author of *Something Wicked This Way Comes*

I cuss let me reach across the world, clutch
The manes of all the galloping horses
A front's tumbling heat
To bareback challenge
    measures of erasure

I can talk —. Plums
& the flesh sweet
    Trees flowering
In the translation of a day
But dear the day is stained
  Unnecessary death

      Frail the page the honest
    Blank.

Carolyn Srygley-Moore (C Leigh) has authored circa
ten books or chaps; most feature some of her visual art/
photography as well. She has written for the empowerment
of what she calls 'the vulnerable ones,' to include human
beings and animals forced by unfortunate facts (' of the farm
') to endure the impossible. Her books include *Miracles of the
Blog; Ode to Horatio and Other Saviors; Termites Amidst the Milky
Way;* and *For All Of My Beautiful Ghosts*. She prefers love over
unnecessary suffering, and wonders what it is, determining
what suffering is "necessary." She wanders around upstate
New York in the company of her husband, James; and
several fabulous dogs; and a rose dangling like a lit cigarette
from her mouths at all times.

This project was made possible, in part, by generous support from the Osage Arts Community.

Osage Arts Community provides temporary time, space and support for the creation of new artistic works in a retreat format, serving creative people of all kinds — visual artists, composers, poets, fiction and nonfiction writers. Located on a 152-acre farm in an isolated rural mountainside setting in Central Missouri and bordered by ¾ of a mile of the Gasconade River, OAC provides residencies to those working alone, as well as welcoming collaborative teams, offering living space and workspace in a country environment to emerging and mid-career artists. For more information, visit us at www.osageac.org

Osage Arts Community